Charles Cullen 74

DESMOND EGAN SELECTED POEMS

For Dick

a pleasure to meet you

– come over to Ireland soon!

warmly

Desmond Egan

(1 April 96 Queen's College)

Books by DESMOND EGAN

Poetry

Midland (1972)
Leaves (1974)
Siege! (1977)
Woodcutter (1978)
Athlone? (1980)
Seeing Double (1983)
Snapdragon (1983, 1992)
Poems for Peace (1986)
A Song for My Father (1989)
Peninsula (1992)

Collected Poems (1983, 1984)
Selected Poems Edited by Hugh Kenner (1992)

In Translation

Terre et Paix French/English (1988)
Echobogen Dutch /English (1990)
Quel Sole Storno Italian/English (1992)

Prose

The Death of Metaphor Selected Prose (1990, 1991)

Critical Studies

Desmond Egan: The Poet and his Work Ed. Hugh Kenner (1990)
Desmond Egan: A Critical Introduction by Brian Arkins (1992)

DESMOND EGAN
Selected Poems

Selected and with an Introduction by
HUGH KENNER

1992
CREIGHTON UNIVERSITY PRESS
THE KAVANAGH PRESS

U.S. edition published by
Creighton University Press
2500 California Plaza
Omaha Nebraska 68178 USA

Overseas edition published by
The Goldsmith Press Ltd.
Newbridge Co. Kildare Ireland

Library of Congress Catalog Card Number: 92-073298
ISBN USA: 1-881871-03-7 paper
ISBN EUROPE: 1-870491-85-8 paper

CONTENTS

For
Viv
and
Kate
and
Bébhinn
with
love

INTRODUCTION
Hugh Kenner

AT ABOUT the age (51) when Yeats was celebrating "a terrible beauty," Desmond Egan was recalling a Paris bar with Sam Beckett,

> our navigator our valiant necessary wanderer to the edges
> of this interpreted world

Yeats, you see, obligated by the 1916 occasion, felt obligated also to coin an indelible phrase. But the "Buddha's emptiness" of such a phrase lies open to catlike parody: hence O'Casey's "A terrible beauty is borneo," rhyming with some "dawn of a wonderful moment" that was never noticed, let alone celebrated. Whereas Beckett was a "navigator", yes, "valiant", yes, a "wanderer", yes, and his world was, yes, the "interpreted" one where we need all our wits yet cannot even feel sure how many steps comprise the stair we're climbing. Egan feels free to be accurate.

He also feels free to omit punctuation, a freedom observable since his earliest work. Like The Great Phrase, punctuation in Ireland marks an obligation toward a celebrated spoken rhythm. "It ruined many a man the same horses," said Davy Byrne in Ulysses, and "the precision of the dropped comma" was soon remarked on. You're hearing Davy Byrne not pause after "man". Whereas Egan writes,

> cyclamen and gladioli linger at the shuttered front
> the weir still breaks in quietness it says Eugene
> and by the lockhouse of Maganey I sat down and wept
> having thought you just as immortal

- an easy one, since the linebreaks take care of three pauses, so the only comma we miss is the one after "quietness". Scanning, though, to insert its pause, we see each word: "still" and "quietness" and "says," for instance. We may even hear Eliot's,

> By the waters of Leman I sat down and wept

then measure a distance from the Psalmist's waters of Babylon via Leman to the lockhouse of Maganey. It's not a diminishing distance: we weep where we must. Meanwhile Egan's verse frees him and all his readers from obligations to Irish cadence.

He is the first Irish poet to have broken free from the need to sound "Irish": to manufacture some way of sounding "Irish." The matter of Ireland comes in almost casually: as it does for a man who drives a car there, and has not only English and Irish but German, French, Spanish, Greek ... (There Joyce did lead, having let us know, in his gone Gaelic-League days, that there were more than two tongues in the world.)

> June and the Boyne walks Leeson Street Avanti
> rows pubs a caravan of seas Killiney
> wine and chips the Burren parties girl friends
> *Lets go* coffee sorting the 'phone the Renault
> family factory bodies letters Celbridge music
> It's BEAU-TIFUL silences driving a smile misery
> and sheer joy

Well, "walks" has to be a noun, and "rows" must rhyme with "blouse" not "hose;' and do "silences" drive a "smile", or is "driving" one more isolate noun? Yes, English can be as curious as Homeric Greek. And that's the texture an Egan poem is made of.

What can be very curious, finally, is the interplay between what we see on the page and what we find ways to voice. In a poem like "Hitchhiker" Egan pushes that to the limit: two poems, one in italics, on the same page. No way to voice them simultaneously; no way, even, to follow them simultaneously. The convention is the monkish manuscript with its marginalia; except that here the marginalia on the right assert a maddening continuity-

> *by gar it's grand*
> *grand*
> *let's see now*

what were we discussing
ah yes
hurling
hurling
hurling

-while on the left the Hitchhiker is showing Polaroid snaps,

one of the wife
shot accidentally dead in a bank at 25
two of his First Communion daughter: yesterday was
the only time since that she cried (he said to the photos)
when he farmed her out to the neighbours
along with the collie dog

No way to utter the two lobes of that. It's all (literally) unutterable.
Enough. Go browse.

COLLECTED POEMS
(1983)

Drawing by Charles Cullen

INTRODUCTION

owned by some neighbours you never meet
a hungry mongrel lopes in the gate of morning   *my room is*
to the backdoor sniffing sharp nose sniff   *awake since seven*
poking into the bin without a lid
any   *the usual record*
anything to eat?

                                                 coffee snorting elsewhere

music floats from this very study as
his teeth flitter through cellophane   *delph sounds*
hurrying sparing no time at the
paper leavings   *a voice*

I cannot stop him   *and out there*
scattering the waste on the tarmac   *over the wire the lawn*
                                           a swift loops two

and scooting with a look back   *thoughts and*
jumping over the grid becoming one with
that same fieldscape the maybush the   *somewhere unseeable*
immemorial skies   *a bird sings centuries*

sloping out into the future

MIDLAND
(1972)

Drawing by Brian Bourke

MIDLAND

a house steamed down the horizon afternoon
the bog sea calm
flat as drainwater the swells of browns rising
to where quiet mountains of cloud sheered ranging away
    like another dimension

and gulls wandered searching in space for their souls

NETTLES

decadent harvest ripening emerald
in silences of moon and the night you
thrum with acid power just to produce
that wrinkly toppling crop
sting-fruited fanatically baited
in treacherous luxuriance
waving the bite of each touch
only to guard your nothing

green rash!   growth
of graveyards dumps and every wilderness
I have seen you sunless one
spread elsewhere spread
down the waste places of the soul

NEAR HERONS TOWN MARCH 19TH

one lark escaping up
above hills that huddled
like the crowd after mass

no river — only furze
bursting crocus round a thornbush
where brown sacks: two fox cubs
minus tails had been hung
updown
still grinning through their teeth

GLENCOLMCILLE 1972

(For Kevin Swan)

then we were standing on the top
its boggy surface yielding underfoot

there was cold from a salmon sea   and mist
over the valley we were passing through

our breaths hung too whisped above it
making it somehow ours I thought

but it was hard to talk
hard to be consoled

better to find the track scramble down
before it got too dark

we still had to pitch a tent
somewhere
under the silent mountain

THUCYDIDES AND LOUGH OWEL

teal
poised on ice
             above the lake's throb

             this blue translucence
             flexing across rocks

                            frozen sprays of fern

             — remind me of your History
             for if the stretched town is become
             part of nature   so
             are your sentences

like gulls they cry
down the cold shores

CLARE: THE BURREN

I.

worn cloud has torn from
turfbank hills which
razor the horizon

above Ballyvaughan one currach
pricks
      the blue space filling overflowing them

and through the draped shadows
a turlough of leaked sunlight
discovering mooncolourings

a dog's bark
fades from nowhere   someone
following three insect cows
carries like its sound

while everything a January moment
catches
its
breath

II.

the redheaded schoolboy (farmer's son)
shyly led the way   across
a livid wilderness of limestone
striated with the ogham of ages
and there it stood
                    the great dolmen!

tipping-out from supporting flags
one massive lintel tons
of jagged uncorroded rock
balanced so austerely it scarcely touched
those gnarled flanges

limestone rising upward
lifting itself — rough parthenon —
beyond itself
skied
pointing away from
the Burren the restless seas

and from the corpses it covered
(Claremen's bones?)
their lint of flesh filtered
like sea stiffened into that stone
hewed
bevelled above them thousands of years ago
yesterday

FOR ALL WE KNOW

(Sung by Billie Holiday)

Sweetheart the night is growing old
Sweetheart
                    my love is still untold

like the scent of withered gardenia
or the vague shine on an old 78
something of youth lingers
in that tired voice
                              whitefaced now
as death — her last lover —
fondles her throat
and that youth
                    that life
                                   all life
becomes goodbye

THE PURSUIT OF DIARMAID AND GRAINNE

I. Diarmaid's Dilemma

her hand
   on my shoulder
her hair
   in my face
her eyes
   in my eyes
my heart
   in a race

II. Gráinne Speaks

something you say unthinkingly sometimes
can chord the shadows of your words
surprising my most silent places
with a suddenness of music

or the desperate tenderness of your eyes
unknown to you as secretly
may haze me in their shallows

and sometimes in your smile all moons collapse
like ancient bones in the light of day

III. Words of the seer Diorraing

You must follow Gráinne Diarmaid
and your death will come of it
and 1 think it an evil thing

but you must follow Gráinne

►

IV. Fionn's Lament

while in your clasping arms sleeping he lies
alone I lie and watch a lonely star
thinking that as it signals from afar
Gráinne you see it glistening — like my eyes

V. The Pursuit

she told him then how the rabbit
runs runs the steely meadow grass
into one path —
a maze which always he follows
even when the scent of death hangs there
as a weasel cuts towards him
and crazed the rabbit scurries
those windings over and back
racing his frenzy   finally waiting
for the killer to saunter up
only crying
when teeth probe dip

whimpering crying for ages
to the relentless eyes

all this she described   the tide
creeping furrowed sands carrying
night
        towards
                them

*VI. Diarmaid dying**

I want to say *You*
but no word
could speak your fingers
your sway in my arms' silence

or your face turning

---

* According to the ancient legend Gráinne, wife of Fionn Mac Cumhail (the archetypal Irish hero, leader of the Fenians) forced Diarmaid to elope with her. Fionn pursued them around Ireland and the chase eventually ended with the death of Diarmaid and Gráinne.

THE NORTHERN IRELAND QUESTION

two *wee girls*
were playing tig near a car ...

how many counties would you say
are worth their scattered fingers?

FOR JOHN BERRYMAN

(Because I love so much
I lose so much — Tao*)

riveted girders blur of carfaces —
the bleary amused eyes eye
their last
                no embrace no hold:
he folds his worn glasses places them on the ledge and
straightens to be shoved
                out

        bridge-steel still
cold in his hurtling fingers

so simple after all
this final wounding openness
this brief suspension
while he brings throbbing like a stripped nerve
all his kingdom buckling down together
smaller and falling smaller
all his americas
into the river-tarmac
(Are there tears in his eyes?
Are there tears in my eyes?)
one last breath
pluming — like Gabriel's message — out of his lips
                                                ▶

---

* Version by Michael Hartnett (Published by New Writers' Press, 1971).

to flower
        to ripple away
chopping into the thought-knurls
slowly sinking sinking deeper
Ha ha alas so long Berryman
Christ - who knew the fall the jerk -
save us all

what's left now this whiskey-bitterness
downed in one smarting gulp but
burrow into the hospital paper telly?

not to think of a kingdom
dangling like a bottle in the empty waters
and eyes the unclosed staring upwards
towards the lighted the innocent skies

DIALOGUE

there is very little I want really -
a stone cottage on the edge of a lake
darkened with woods
(there would have to be woods)
and of course some someone special
we could live there quietly with the birds

you don't want much my friend
just more than anyone has ever managed

even the birds

LEAVES
(1978)

Drawing by Charles Cullen

ALONG THE BOYNE

you were ahead
your path bruising gently
into the entanglement of grasses that
fume of blossoming weeds nettles daisies
and one bloodred poppy skirted
by the narrow track
while down to the right the weired river
relaxed like the grass agagain
(hiding as always its salmon)
to slow forever over curving
into foam rhythms
I followed on that way secret
and delicate as the circles by the reeds

until you were there below
turning smiling in the flowered gown
nettle-burned thumb still to your lips
waiting   where the path stopped

June 72

THE OTHER SIDE

I opened the door
                     a delicate presence
of air and birds
the casual Liffey

of autumn colours
my serious trees
and a daisy or two still saying *Love me Love me*

and all this morning diamond in grass
someone with summer floating into the past

THE TUNNELS OF JUNE

up the tunnels of June
he drove her drove
as light shattered
splashing on the screen
and green shadow
closed each side
of this otherworld
where everything teemed
mile upon mile of
profusion struggling
like the lost —
absorbing their passage
as quiet does notes

and the way that she flitted
before he could know

a soaked rose
deepened above the gravel streaming
by her orphic window

EARLY MORNING LATE JULY

trout feeding along the river
taking in hinged whips . . . still

no matter what I do
squinting shortsightedly
cupping hands against the riverimages

I can see nothing

more than a scuffle the questing
nooses of water

though you can *feel* them out there
eyes set set mouths
floating and flicking

while the hour-flies
little specks of mortality
drift drift quietly on
from everywhere

rises are like fingerprints —
listen

THE FLY IN THE TOWER

was a thorn of noise
in from the river bzz banging my lamp
irritating bzz desperate
as if the room were a web
BZZ
inviting outrage
like an autumn wasp —

so that I left the chair
I left the desk lashing out
and again!
hardly feeling the hit

but the fly
had skidded into a wall
and fallen and folded a
spot on the quilt

QUIET

everything reforming accommodating
as a mind to its cut

— but what had I done:

two web legs
slowed once and closed
in that prenatal curtsy while
fragile and practical as a girl
the ribbed —so lovely —winglets
betrayed their background

▶

and imagine the rainbows
of prism retinae their poem opal ...

loss oh loss —

but things were irrevocable
as as the deaths we all live
loving and losing   graceless
I bent to shuffle
it hide it away
too

the fly crouched

Author's Note: Around this time I was living in a tower in Newbridge, Co. Kildare; the *Lady of Shalott* echo in paragraph two is intentional.

REQUIEM

music you loved has filled like autumn with sadness
and places we used to be I can hardly bear
flowers are less than flowers days are of-darkness
something fell like a leaf when you went away

THREE SONGS FROM *The Story of Oisín**

1. Fionn's Song

horse in the window
ashes of a dawn
whisper to the ceiling
someone's gone

hoofbeats of morning
hollow as a room
birds of unknowing
someone's gone

cold of old gables
where the wind waits
crystal on a table saying
gone away

past of a packed case
snapped   a gate swung
o horse stone mornings —
gone

---

*The Songs of Niamh, Fionn and Oisín are from an unfinished music sequence.

2. Oisín's First Song

the appleblossoms waltzed   white roses
joined hands to dance around the wall
and from a window wisps of music
lingered like sunlight on the lawn
and yet this loveliness
was less than your smile ....

across the fields the river walking
talked to the bridge the listening hills
two birds went swooping gorgeous upstream
passing our path beside the mill
and yet this loveliness
was less than your voice

I saw you running   all my thoughts
zig-zagged for joy like butterflies
— your look laugh of forgetmenots
your reaching arms your singing eyes ....
love all your loveliness
is more than my heart

3. Niamh's Song

talk with me Love one last time
down that river of old dreams
turn and smile your tragic smile
goodbye Oisín goodbye me

what turned wrong: I know and don't
— you used make this new world real
love what will we do alone?
goodbye Oisín goodbye me

now you'll turn into the songs that you sang?
now our summer fall in leaves:
kiss and break but don't look back
goodbye Oisín goodbye me

all the places that are you in my thoughts
fade! like hawthorn after spring
no two loved as much — and lost
goodbye Oisín goodbye me

SUNSET EVENING

the light had a strange intenseness
like the last note of a lovesong

it made different space
where things stood vivid and inescapable:

another green in the green by the hedgerow
out my door   shock of the wall's pallor
patient trees the livid pink
of a rotivated lawn . . . all those facts
draining (it is night now)
into hills of quiet

with one bird warbling occasionally

the way it used to be

COWSLIP COWSLIP

last weekend I saw what I half dreaded seeing
again: it wasn't cowslips that stopped me dead

but one *gorgeous* evening far side of Celbridge
oak trees a city train ditches of *Devil's Bread*

and the waves of that meadow deep as the June seemed
where someone was picking bending her long head

like a cowslip
                   then straying towards the car in the gateway
leaving everything unsaid

Devil's Bread: wild parsley

DIARY

the thirtieth of a wet May
so different from last years!

hawthorn along the hills below Slane —
bluebell Celbridge — our supermarket of sun —
Killiney the colour of Smithwicks —
and the slow warm evenings dying into Leeson Street —

tonight at my bookcase
new rain was sneaking like weeks across glass
when I just happened to notice the stained diary
1973 inked on its spine put away
like an old book of poems in a leather binding

STILL LIFE WITH ASHTRAY

after the few short hours its morning bowl
was littered with a surprising collection of butts

stubbed and twisted they lay mute arguments
as if the light that had burned to each was a life forced
out among the ash and charred matches

beside them in primary colours the matchbox
which clattered emptily like a toy when I shook it

the two chairs were still pulled out as if someone had just left

smokesmell

a packet of cigarettes forgotten on the mantlepiece

QUESTION WITHOUT
A QUESTION MARK

already well on the way to November
the river carries its confetti of this year's leaves
leaves those very leaves we watched springing
the day before yesterday

epic movement of tired waterlogged histories they pass
yielding as dreams I suppose must to reality

so where's the point finally
of plans of loves of regrets of achievements all the false
      colours
of conversations in pubs before Closing

what matter
          soldier on .... look
the oaks are throwing a fireworks display
and *a few little fishes* widening rings through the traffic

FOREST

(For Sam Beckett)

it's *anything* still this shadowbright floor
dream deep scream deep *where we live*
matter shuffles forms skip the flowers may be birds
chiming down the marigold the owl moon's courses

where we live ha ha
lost *where we live*

SIEGE!
(1976)

Photograph by courtesy of Pat Maxwell Agency

I TTTHE WWWWARRANT

under siege no doubt themselves the Guards
drove across the face of the whole 26
— even the undiscovered parts —
peering into houses as if they were cars

and swooped on a few quarters by night Bang
O lente lente currite noctis equi
Bang Bang Bang Bang Bang
to screeching windows *Open up*
Open Up it's the Police
come in sly battalions at three in the morning
like tenders of Black and Tans

to tramp in pairs by more than one sleepy father
by more than one typist
shivering in her nightgown hand on the latch
their capped faces the navy uniform of their voices
cutting upstairs and down like flashlights

if you took a peep out the bedroom blinds
the street was thronged with dark unmoving shapes
cordoned off by low Gárda Síochána tones
and the intermittent thud and revv. of cars as if a Super.
were having the whole neighbourhood interned without trial
Into the van please

long after they melted down the streetlights of dawn
the guilt of having been accused
would lie around like the torn floorboards of *Nite Bite*
Chips Burgers Chick'n Snax

or like the warrant no one chanced asking for

VI AND HERE IS THE NEWS *ARSA* *THE MONUMENT*

the only weekend before another by-election
in the depressed West we all love
suddenly as the splitting headache which spread which outscaled
any sandwich of policeman — politician — priest
even seasoned with Yard psychology-mustard
(Why pay more?)
a revolver was being dropped

                              another

onto the plot
to lodge there
like the Northern voice
the bullhorn answers

before the whiteness of faces
stumbling in turn into that red November
the blue violence of flashbulbs
and microphones rearing like snakes

Let us go then, you and I

you could hear the night's telegraph wires
whinnying like snipe above the Square
above the hardware shop
the private and public houses
the monument to Father Prendergast

so that next breakfast the entire country
might skim over headlines and blow-ups louder than a Kelloggs box

►

and we could adjust them in our evening screens where interviewees
*Currtainly Currtainly (*no *confusion source of renewals)*
dipped and jostled tail-up like hungry swans
down the oily waters of *Law and Order*

and while drums of celluloid queued like Nato troops
and chance turned into words turned into paper
Táim-se im' chodhladh is ná dhúisigh mé
the three prisoners marched after fate:
heavy sedation
the Bahamas
solitary

far from the lorries of commerce rolling up and down the Naas road.

Táim-se ... I am asleep and don't waken me (old Irish song).

WOODCUTTER
(1978)

Photograph of Giacometti sculpture courtesy of Thomas Gibson Gallery

TENTED BY THE EMBALSE
ON JUNE 21

maybe the lap of anguish
could sink in that liquid bed

pitched like canvas along the bottoms
with lauds of a lark over our head—?

but the ripples were muttering *La Muerte*
La Muerte La Muerte
the mud at one's feet clouded

red
and the pine scent of yesterday evening
—plunging—I noticed was dead now

---

* Embalse: artifical lake in Spain.

CANCER

Monday's call his first in ages
we were too nice—
awkwardly tender as when the train
doors are being shut
                    right along the platform

—and he knew it well
Only a few months God help him

how does the river look now
which he used drive along in the morning
and leave absently dangling a stethoscope?
how do the trees the far hills?

and people
          old patients who seem suddenly to have won
health like a Silver Circle prize?

—too familiar yet different? like clothes
that don't quite fit any more   the whole living world
a hotel in the off-season

only the thin end of love is more real
than long fields greening with their last spring

the delicate cold rain is inexpressibly beautiful

THE HERON

another year another afternoon
another sunny cloud in an October sky
and vehicles suddenly glinting like flickknives
over back in pursuit along one horizon of grass

overcoat round my legs I was sitting
like an invalid in the car
scanning the same old different river
an almost unmoving road the leaves the crimples
with which I used to walk

down in the water slithering at the weir
the heron waits

MORNING FROM KNOCKAULIN

remember the dew how white it was?
the flashes of plastic at Allen in the bluish distance?
remember the smokefibres slowly untangling
over the midlands little cattle
lying down the fields and the fox
treading startled turning
into the gorse at the royal fort

overlooking Kilcullen?
                                        down there you had
housewives with the radio on   children
crouching to their lessons men
busy as the sand lorry—a Dinky toy plying the road

remember?

WOODCUTTER

it's not good to go back

                              below the stone arches
the Boyne ran shallow too full of what is past

cut of its skyline cleaner than ever
landlocked like the millwheel

and the bank where one had to climb down
the hanging tree stump
still there where I used to widen barbed wires
to let someone through

couldn't stay long

                        uphill a silhouette
was urging a chainsaw slicing for firewood
out of old hulks

UNDER LONDON

darkness and banks of light
and in that spread of blocks
going on going off a human galaxy

someone
whom once—

one soul I know
somewhere out there
near enough as the sudden past the
few years gone

no point in scanning the streets foolishly driving along

gone like the moan of a plane into the night

June and the Boyne walks Leeson Street *Avanti*
rows pubs a caravan of seas Killiney
wine and chips the Burren parties girl friends
Let's go coffee sorting the 'phone the Renault
family factory bodies letters Celbridge music
It's BEAU-TIFUL silences driving a smile misery
and sheer joy

as close as far away
as the lights of London from the Hackney marshes
where the tent was pitched sagging in a summer drizzle

where you could lament in the deeper city
quiet for everything that passes so fast it
becomes fully real only by memory

the track where a tent has stood

the Hackney marshes

SUNDAY EVENING

hands in jeans along Dollymount I don't see
the slow line of the wave breaking far
out under Howth in mist a Tír na nOg I don't see
the long strand quiet as another sky
nor the seasun the wrack dead things a saturated beam

—but you who are not there
sitting any more legs crossed on a sand dune
picking at chips with musical fingers to laugh
deeper than the wine that *This is LOVE-ly*
while the sparse grass blows

forever as I pass

WHIT 1977

beautiful the swooping finch I never saw
before had become in a wince little more than
that wag of dead feathers
half fluttering on my mirror road

because I was driving fairly fast
somewhere there is no forgiveness to be asked

too familiar gone
its touch on the flyspattered windscreen
muffled and gentle as the thud of five years

onto the consciousness I go smoking towards
in a hit and run car

V—

I will draw inwards I will leave distractions
standing like milkbottles at the mornings front gate
humbly I will glut my pen deep in the ink of beginning
I will not answer the letter I must answer
nor lift any phone nor read nor open the hollow door
not even if the world I love shout
I will switch on no transistor
but extravagantly crumple the tooth pages into my basket
forehead heating eyes a bit last night sore
and extraordinarily webbed as if with dissipation
I will not think about hands or cold feet of any kind
at this hard desk where day is shivering like a board
nor will I walk the wet road yet though that would be nice
but let it all fade awhile away like a gust of rain
while I write typewrite examine coolly
with Shakespearean indifference to any audience but my
     own

I will spend ages allow many a lorry of spray
to rattle forever past on coin wheels
only finally to scrap nearly everything
with—pardon me—no attempt at defence no excuse
when I stand up at last stretching in disappointment

not to have hit on the poem that I want the lines o even the
     few
that might a moment of always catch you hold you

ALMOST FEBRUARY

Moloney shouts a *Ho* and raises one hand
flying by on his motorbike to work

and the cry lingers
like an image cut in light
as the birds and hills of clouds the tractor the fullness
take over again

and even though the radio has already carried
The North with a man shot dead in his bed at 4 a.m.
slaughter in Lebanon
the heartless Russian grab at Angola
—so many including a few from home who didn't make
    this spring—
like cold air into my cottage

in spite of all that or partly because of it or whatever
I make myself a promise once more
to love every minute of this morning coming up like a
    snowdrop
this day this fresh time
simple as joy that is also old as the hills

and let my shout back after the echoes

LATE BUT! ONE FOR EZRA

I cannot take you off the lawns of the mental home
called after St. Elizabeth where you wandered twelve years
and sat behind doors behind doors waiting for callers no
nor be of any use now on your release back into the world
of 1958 *incurably insane but harmless*
I'M TALKING ABOUT EZRA POUND

my hands are tied by time's red tape there is really nothing
   I can do
to try to dissuade you *il miglior fabbro* as I dearly would

from lapsing into the wire cage of silence
from *the enormous tragedy* of your own dream
shimmering forever unreached like the fields of Pisa
I'm talking about Ezra Pound

it is too late now to attend your last reading
at 86 of Marianne's *What Are Years?*
(no poem out of all your own)—
though the grizzled voice the eyes that had been scourged
the mortal raggedy tongues of white hair
seem real as your hat this minute
I'm talking about Ezra Pound

there is nothing nothing anyone can do

                ►

---

incurably insane ... from the official document of release.

unless maybe put it on record that even what is Jewish in
    us all
forgives with a wave of the hand one who was years too
    sensitive
a continent too brave and never for yourself
so that your own U.S. of promise trailed off on the skyline
    like a sentence

too late too late for a gesture it doesn't matter any more
but it does to me

who join with the priest in the Gregorian chant
    at your funeral
In paradisum
deducant te angeli
rest troubled Hercules! your best labours shine like new
    words
the remainder as with anyone else doesn't count

these few lines from my time that would have been worse
    only for you

I'm talking about Ezra Pound

NOT ON THE COURSE

(For Ned Flynn)

first snowdrops today! three weeks late
tinkling silently by the path inside the old iron gate the
    good place
as if they had always been there

but maybe Brecht and Co. are right
and one shouldn't be writing this rural stuff
or bothering in cancery times with things like
a high crow in wind shooting the heavens

or getting just slightly annoyed as this afternoon
at being dominated by the same hill
much less go stalking to identify a swoop of birds
which dropped piping up the ploughed field like wildduck

such things can hardly matter any more
than rain stars falling down your double glazing
—they are like Latin and Greek which most parents agree
ought to be dropped from the Syllabus

LET'S GO

some days leave a recognizable
touch on the face?
some years?

happened we met again an afternoon
that reminded *me* of another Mays ago

extravagances of green and cowslips the ditches jungles
sky halfhid in leaves holding sun like the railway bridge
where we leaned out to a train coming thundering shaking
     everything
faces lives rattling down the steel tracks for keeps

two years
filed in this face I used to know
the stone warm on my palms
two full years day in day out
held there without me   as the remainder will
O heavens! is't possible!
oneself one's failures too?
recognized as a father does one of his souls in a child . . .

Let's go

the tracery of a voice saying nothing
as important as the scissors glances quick frowns
the ghosts

a carload of students still cheers down the empty summers

is that how it passes?
is that exactly how it passes?

ATHLONE?
(1980)

Photograph by Leo Mahon, Athlone

ATHLONE?

as from a garden of original grace and sin something

of twisty lanes of oblique streets
of voices calm as the landscape
a walk a spiritual accent
lingers in fingerprints everywhere

makes me persist an interviewer of sorts
dogged with simple questions my earphones squeaking
cop yourself on because all art
contains an element of the ridiculous

still
elbows on the shiny stone my soul without ambition
keeps trying to open a door on a street or two
the light the footsteps the brief voices
that pull at our amniotic fluids that fix our horoscopes
more than any stars

and while the town that is only my town flows
by with its river rhythms
shimmery so slow and dignified with lives I

will glide like a crow up the narrow casual ways
up through shopdoors and windows the many storeys
of an idea shared like a zodiac
by faces that turn like gables
by friends by neighbours
by singsongs from pubs curling out in smoke
uphill towards my own home

▶

bred born and reared inside me it tolls
more slowly now turning all into afternoons
with something of that sad echo of the Barrack chimes bringing
together in quiet as if everything were waiting
the sweetshops people roads the Battery hills of the past
my Connaught Street

angelus of the small place we discover
has left us in exile everywhere else

someone waves from the front door and turns back in

CROW ODE

drift cawing to light your black fires always
round the Protestant trees behind my youth

gabble like gossips through the morning ceiling
seesaw with curiosity on a day's clotheslines
or swivel from the sky of roofs or echo
like an unfinishable poem round the vans in the bakery yard and
down Pipe Lane galvanising its gates

mock leisurely at our schooldays
floating beyond the railings above the canal
or stepping like a shopkeeper in the lushness we have to leave
beneath the oaks of a day or two

ruffle slowly through winds the lingering of rain
unloved as perch or the rabbit yet surviving
accepting your fate as tinkers do

even to blink unsurprised at our red pellet
punctures on that vinyl breast

then scatter like families forever through the dusk branches
catching us only in years with your strange singing
nightingale of our town

ECHO ARCHES
(for Peter Nijmeijer)

it's July and
you delay with two returns
at the bottom of the Library steps
just to take in the river wide and full
with boats and the dark light of water shifting
into shallows holding the promenade of trees

from huge feet the railway bridge
spreads its gulls' wings this side
of the pike island where someone lived

maybe the soul grows at such moments
borrowing becoming the swifts that skim
delighted under echo arches

with my bike the Leinster side
seems to wait for things to happen as
a few drops sift onto the
unread books

FLOODS

like an accent the water
drawls all over Clonown our estate
a tideless sea of cold simplifying everything the
cottages moored here and there
with barns and ditches the wind in a galvanised shed
and the road itself questions
while we walk at his pace my father and I
up the bogs
to see the floods

and talk through the greyness as little birds
nip about in loops of hope
by elder and sallies the thorn stripped of peashooter haws
passing landmarks like the cement seat
empty as usual the slow bend and
holding only wavelets an iron gate
that must have been forged down our way

people and their stories a lifetime
emerge with houses as he goes
paying respects unlike Philoctetes with humour
to the Halligans Hugheses Logans Wards
who often dropped into the shop
carrying like bicycle lamps their island ways
Dunnings Fallons the Derwins Henrys
the Floating Palace that never got finished
and Mickey Egan the cardplayer who nearly lived forever

someone splashes in a tractor from Mass a
girl with her pram changes wellingtons at the tide's edge
and Mossie cycles by cheerily carrying milk
saluting being saluted there are
spits of blood where he stretched his throat to Sunday ►

reminding me of Inis Mean and back in Clare
all those faces austere as the bushes

down the Shannon fields a houseboat
moves in fantastic peace
                              the swans have gathered again
they dip and call swing round towards us
like souls of a tribe implicit as land

it is time to turn back for town
waiting there raised like docks
under the mountains of slate cloud

MATINEE IN THE RITZ

(For Tomás and Eugene)

as if *the pictures* were on we
lean my brother and I to the balustrade
of the ninepenny balcony suspended
above the stalls and pit of noise
in those airless cinema smells that reassure
with the background music the draughts of doorlight
the only thing ever I would never be late for

then *deadly!* the curtains two
concertinas of promise glowing instantly surging
upwards as a frame splits across them
in the new breathless darkness
where another theme clashes out
with all the dangerous certainty of art

inspired by the steady beam of lightdust
and tense as celluloid we gape
while all the particles flicker dart together the
cells of our atom stabbing
excitedly like the usherette's torch

the crook
the hero

and later retreat down the spiral of lino
to emerge blinking into Sunday unreality
cold a breeze the bridge for home
leaving the neon arteries

pulsing always on the other side

LEAVING THE CONVENT SCHOOL

aroundabout noon the escapees
would burst in every direction from the one archway
that fell behind along with the
nuns and sums the high roller blinds
and Black Babies' boxes

out into the revolutionary streets
chanting in gangs
We got our holidays and
We don't care
swinging by the straps those useless schoolbags

over the soft tar of summer

MRS. NED

she would waddle out from their stone kitchen
gently on slippers her bandaged leg
giving inwards as if under the soft
bulk in the navy shopcoat
usually calling back at some of the *childer*
poor Marion never too far away
or Barney Thomas our pal

every year she'd have their shop window in flowers
with candles and a Sacred Heart for the procession
and my mother cried a long time
the evening Mrs. Ned died

O'CONNELL ST.
(For all the Brocks)

a very last wave as if for keeps back
towards my Aunt out at the door of no. 10
and the Stanley kitchen cooling on my face
then stepping on the way home along the
iron grilles at Kenny's at Connaughton's
an eerie feeling
                        there and yet kindof not
treading air a challenge my sister would dodge

I'd often stand in the middle to look
at the paper rubbish cigarette boxes etc.
lollipop sticks halfchewed wafers a shoe
inevitably a comb and the perfection of a coin you couldn't reach
days lost or maybe dropped for luck
town life writ small just as in
the *pawn* window down Bastion Street

rattling across was delicious but dying a little

if the Guinness horse and float were around
that trap would be lifted exposing the cellar
and as every barrel dropped onto the sack of sand it
tolled hollow wood visceral
as the ice cream taste of death

BAYLOUGH

computer digits on the petrol pump
blur into themselves into the bog
when you look out from Monksland Hill and see
that wideness the browns and ochres all autumn colours
tiding away taking the eye in mutations in flat ranges
towards a bluish haze of distances
our sunken forest level as a steppes maybe less
obvious but no less beautiful it
creates as a canal does its own scale
a midland one satisfying as any seascape
a sudden feast on the Galway road reminding me
that I am a citizen of no mean country and *anytime*
the vast sky the clouds will do for cliff
over our motionless sea

HEALION'S

one step and the rattling latch
would let you into that smell of ice cream
the deep hum of a fridge

and the belljars sunny motionless
waiting like daisies to be discovered
and bars of chocolate in open boxes
and cellophane cigarettes

the small messages of a life

mostly we had to wait for Mrs. Healion
while a threepenny bit hardened in the hand and
the curtains turned gingham before they moved

her frown was like the sound of a wafer

and frown she did
at the sight of the football boots the ball

ENVOI

saying goodbye for the umpteenth time the
mind like a pensioner drifts on a favourite walk
up the living road towards the bogs
that flood and colour everywhere

no doubt it could catch
this side of the tidiness of Curnabull those
obvious moments along the Shannon
but that's a bit much just now
there being so little one can cope with

so I go up and up the same way in hope
as far as the cross river
lean over the bridge and
join the weeds the ancient shadowings of water

somewhere out there
like a hint of smoke on the breeze Clonmacnois
rises in thought a graveyard wide with unheard goodbyes
the skygoats are whinnying high
high in a summer evening
cutting sad happy celtic circles over our heads

the hedges have greened I am walking very slowly
listening to my father

SNAPDRAGON
(1983)

Drawing by Brian Bourke

AN GHAOTH ANDEAS

(Focail do'n bhfonn: An Ghaoth Andeas)

Tá ghaoth ag séideadh ar mo shaol monuar
An ghaoth andeas len a deóra fuara.

An Iúil anois scuabtha óm'bhlian go brách.
Tá mo shúile go leanúnach ag caoineadh.

O d'imigh mo ghrá ar an Domhnach Dubh
I gcasadh a dlaoi, gan slán, gan phóg,
Thuit fuiseog mo gháire dá tost go deo,
Bhris an ghrian; rug an ghaoth ar m'óige.

Mar ghlanadh an lae a bánú, seal:
Ach mar leóithne sa spéir straic sí léi, mo gheal.

A Bhainríoghain ríogach, Miongháire mo chroí,
O fill, is ná fág mé mar néall sa ghaoith.

THE SOUTH WIND
(Words for a traditional Irish tune)
A wind is blowing on my life, alas,
The south wind with its cold drops.

Now July is snatched for good from my year,
My eyes have tears in them.

Since she left -my love- on that black Sunday
In the toss of her hair without kiss or goodbye
The lark of my laughter fell silent forever
Sun broke,the wind blew into my youth.

Her brightness was like the dawning of day
But like a gust of wind she left, my sun.

Impulsive queen! tiny smile of my heart,
O come back and don't leave me like a cloud on the breeze.

PRÉACHÁIN GO GLÓRACH AR AN DÍON ÍSEAL

préacháin go glórach ar an díon íseal

gach áit 'na gcónaím
agus seomra ar sheomra mo theach
á fholmhú díotsa

is eol dom ar thraein chun áit éigin eile thú
ag dul i ndoiléire idir dhá cheann na scríbe méaranna
an mhachnaimh mar thaca faoi do cheann is eol dom
ag teacht orm arís thú: an
bhreith sin chomh bog is chomh géar leis an óige

ag déanamh i láthair na huaire díom
gadaí go fiú i mo theach féin
agus screadann gach ní ag fógairt 'éagsúlachta
agus déanann an oíche tafann
tafann iomrall anbhá

mignonne m'aondóchas deifrigh ar ais chugam tar
ag tuiliú isteach na soilse id' fhochair fuaimeanna
                                        an ghnáthshaoil an
guth adeir *tá sé ceart*

agus an anáil sin féin an aistíl
díreach is an ceol ina thús

Translation of *Crows Are Clamouring* ... by Douglas Sealy.

CROWS ARE CLAMOURING ON THE LOW ROOF

crows are clamouring on the low roof
of everywhere I live
and room by room my cottage
falls empty of you

I know you are on a train to someplace else
blurring between destinations the fingers
of thought balancing your face I know
you are figuring me out again: that
judgment tender and cruel as youth

making me become now a
burglar even in my own house
so that everything begins to scream its otherness
and the night barks
barks

Mignonne my only hope come
flooding in with lights the normal sounds the
voice which says *it's all right*

and that very breath the strangeness
just as the music starts

A RUNDIAMHAIR NACH DTEASTAIONN UAIM A THOMHAIS

a rúndiamhair nach dteastaíonn uaim a thomhais
go brách i léaschriocha do shúl
sna méara ceo úd i gcaoin-imigéiniúlacht éigin i
mbeóla ceisteanna nach féidir a chur bíogann sé umat é
chomh tragoideach doshainmhíníoch le gruaig a léarguis

ar bháisteach ag macallú anuas spéartha ní
féidir liom thú a tharrtháil feasta ód' dhán
a bhaineanns liomsa anois a ghrá

linne! tá aiteas sa smaoineamh
agus ligeann na crainn doileire id' ghlór
duillí uathu ar son duillí eile

féachfad le do shoipriú chugam nós abha d'fhonn
chuile thromluí tuiteamais a shraonadh lem' bheo
            damsa an dorchadais an fhuachta

le do tharraingt anuas nós ceann codhlataigh ar
bhaclainn áit gur féidir linn bheith ag brionglóid arís le chéile

---

Translation of *Mystery* ... by Tomás Mac Siomóin.

MYSTERY WHICH I NEVER WANT TO SOLVE

mystery which I never want to solve
in the horizons of your eyes
in those mist fingers in a gentle far offness in
the lips of unaskable questions it tosses round you
tragic and indefinable as hair o vistas

of rain of echoing down skies I
can no longer save you from your fate
which has now *a ghrá* become my own

ours! the thought is a gladness
and in your voice the obscure trees
yield leaves for other leaves

I will try to cradle you to me like a river to
ward off with my life all the nightmares of falling
and the dance of the dark the cold

to draw you gently as a sleeping head
into the arm where we can dream again together

THROUGH FLURRIES OF WIND AND
THE RAIN

through flurries of wind and the rain I
am reaching again for you
for you

love the summer has blown into clouds leaving
september falling everywhere
the slow rain of defeat

will you remember yet this hour
this patch of river those
sad sycamores filled with their fall?

remember will you
the grey universe moving unseen under fronts
its hollow afternoon sounds
a child crying into the future
and the me of this moment you hardly knew?

through september I am reaching again for you

MISLAYING LOSING LEAVING YOURSELF BEHIND

mislaying losing leaving yourself behind
in some railway paperback your shopping bag a
memo of urgent jobs to be done
the small change of your everydays...you
scatter with a gardener generosity your own
sweet fingerprints aroundabout my world

to lie in surprising corners of the soul
letters sorted by the loving eye

how I admire that in you which magnificently can
drive away with me in talk forgetting
to a wet street the sum total of your belongings!

only a rich soul
could sow such after images and

under the extravagance of those green fingers
love grows love

SEEING DOUBLE
(1983)

Illustration by Alex Sadkowsky

NEEDING THE SEA

in September maybe most: that time
when the earth begins to take over again
something in me gets bogged down and
cries out for the grace of water

there's no need friend to remind me
about the countless whose lives are far from such luxury
about starvation and misery the latest holocaust
of those who never got a dog's chance oh
as I write I can hear the scream of
someone being carefully tortured while others
with their only life blindfolded face into
the high cement wall of one military or another
even the thought like that of Poland becomes
a kind of dying: what that hitcher from the North felt
as he watched the blaze of his cottage

we all know about the houses of hopes blown up blown out
we all bump into the local alcos the druggie
youngsters their adult faces mugged by less than poverty
just off the O'Connell Street of our new towns

is the world which so many miss
realised for them you'd wonder through others
do we carry it for this mongol child that
bucketful of abortions in the sluice room?

I need the sea
my being as if on strike soundlessly cries out
to come on it high above the road I
want to stand on that rock which tells no lies and
feel the grassgreen otherness making the mind reel
see the wide slow gathering of a watershadow rising rising up into

the wash the rush the clatter spreading down a beach
hear the strangely comforting clicking of pebbles

I need
to be consoled by the rush of my own smallness
to swim my soul awhile in the pure space let it go adrift
where one wave can hide the shore

at times I need this deep

forgive me

GOODBYE OLD FIAT

my 127 that had to be towed in
with your rust eczema flaring through the blue

and your leak puddles each side of the floor
your driver's seat with the small tear over a spring
your steering wheel that developed a split
oh and the visor that slowly comes down as one drives
your gears of mud your engine with the rattle
which turned mechanics' heads quicker than a nice girl

along with the flotsam in the back window
I left enough of myself in you even a stranger
will find money probably under the seat and
an ashtray of cigarillo relics I never wanted to empty

pardon me for forgetting your number is it possible
I won't sit in you anymore and watch
through your windscreen my river world
trying to squeeze words out of half hours?

no nor come to think of it drive you
in that thickening silence of a row
nor meet you know who at the station
while you wait in the background like the future

nor park you outside town pubs city pubs
nor steam-in late to school in you the morning after
taking chances belting it across the Curragh

nor forget you on summer days at lovely spots
Knockaulin Hill Moone the Burren in spring

▶

nor curse dangerous-and-lady drivers wildly to you
nor push you on one leg downhill chucking at starting
nor abandon you to the garage like a delinquent
nor scrape your glass clear of the frost
of winter Mondays?

no more will I dump typewriter coat case books letters
on top of everything else in your back seat

I will never be sad
delighted hopeful annoyed browned-off thoughtful
again inside you
who loitered at the background of my life
bringing together like a symbol those last few
so suddenly finished years years
now shaped as definitely as your body and I

wonder will your next driver discovering odds and ends
realise that he has bought a haunted car?

HITCHHIKER

what makes you stop? the empty roadside full of
his middleage a bag in the verge I
leaned to the passenger door he ran and
startling as some forgotten accent on the phone
The North was sitting beside me
    outside Mullingar

his voice softly accepted awful things it held
too much like the travelling bag including
all that had happened yesterday his cottage
    bombed
and smoking up into the Dungannon sky
a decision standing there with daughter and bike
a few arrangements then off on an
    unapproved road
through the long violent darkness the cold
footing it all night for the border

he fished out three polaroid snaps
one of *the wife*
shot accidentally dead in a bank at 25
two of his First Communion daughter: yesterday
    was
the only time since that she cried (he said to the
    photos)
when he farmed her out to neighbours
along with the collie dog

after the killers got life
his Protestant job had been next to go
no hard feelings: what choice had the boss
if he valued his kneecaps or house?

Jack 'n Jill
climb up no hill
but Jack sits down
    anyhow
produces his public
    pipe
a match
hmm
two!
puff
puff
careful
slow
philosophic smoke
puff
puff
pull
cheeks
large black glasses
a gentle smile
good
very good
by gar it's grand
grand
let's see now
what
were we discussing
ah yes
hurling
hurling
hurling
Jim Mackey or Christy

▶

and what could anyone do now? we
gave him a dinner a few bob another
Southern lift out of town left him like a tinker
hanging round a filling station on the Galway
   road
until the mirror swallowed him up

each unique of course
but I think on balance . . .
Ring
huh?
the Sunday lunch
with my three butties
grand lads

no much point adding to this or imposing
some treacherous thought for the day
why must we demand virtue of the poor?
his name was Jim something he used play for
   Tyrone
and what I mostly remember a few weeks later
are the photographs with their adhesive blots

you should take up the
  pipe

grand

grand

grand

HUNGER STRIKER

once again their Birmingham door
thumps shut on everything a time safe
and that eye fills the judas hole to stare at
one more *mick* who refuses *silly bugger*
to take the packet soup preferring to
follow those who starved with grass on their
  mouth

join the queue
wash centuries from the car on Sundays
and you'll never walk alone

the cold is loneliness not moving
like the remains through which a bone might
  push
and the transistor a drip forming dropping
our *peculiarly Irish* lefts and rights
while apathy's hands turn on their quartz
analogue of dying

under the cement windows saracens in
  camouflage
run on rubber through their dustbin empire
with 9 cm. bullets stamped
for export only

further the same road blue
helmets with visors and overtime and plastic
  shields
baton and scatter the south *mé fhéin* included
in the direction of *a jar the tea*
and paddywaggons of faces cruise Wood Quay

top 'em
e puffed it
top 'em
e puffed it
top 'em
e puffed it
top 'em
e puffed it
top 'em
e puffed it
top the bloody lot
e puffed it
well if you ask me I say
cap — no top 'em
e puffed it
and another
and another
that's how many
terrorists I call 'em
another puffed it
how many does that
  make
the last puffed it too

who cares
know wot I mean
know wot I mean
know wot I mean
know wot I mean
know wot I mean
know wot I mean

►

UN-LOCK
UN-LOCK
UN-LOCK H BLOCK
floating down Park Lane a chauffeur's glove
presses and the electric glass fills with reflections
whirring discreetly upwards to its destination

teeth grin like Robertson's golliwogs

wot's yer poison?

* Author's Note re. *Robertson's golliwogs* : I read in a newspaper that British troops in one company in Aden were awarded a Robertson's jam label for every unruly native they shot.

SNOW SNOW SNOW SNOW

like some obvious symbol snow
overnight had sifted everywhere
startling the mind's eyes into seeing again
the field forms the gentle hills of Kildare
and even a bruised sky with its line
of Russian pines the whole thing
a steppes where I began to watch
Mandelstam trudging to the death camp

having to leave a place can make it also
turn different in a day the way
hospital does to someone you knew well
and now this area that had seemed mine
has gone old is marching away on me

but landscapes of course don't matter
anything like people and is it I wonder a fact
that we the ordinary got-at allow too much
to go dulling past as if screened including
even those we love and must leave the
day after tomorrow?

is this the despairing chase of verse?
that handful of pianonotes which can
sink inwards like hot ashes or the old
desolating rush of tenderness squeezing into
tears at some subtitled film why the house of
    morning
tenses this minute like a mousetrap

so what can I do? *nada*
— about the snow dazzling into the kitchen
and round your softness where you stand
briefly dabbing at the mirror
this that eternity

unseeable lapwing
mew of distance and
    otherness

they leave you at the very
    swell
the pure winterdark

everything stripped to itself

a bark

a single light

salt down the apple tree

look for me there
generations away

TWENTY YEARS

(To the memory of Bobby Harkin, R.I.P. 1979)

tatty Wickow! it surprised me
renewing itself in cement bunkers and
the same rocky front where the same wave
peters out flooding in soda into that very
corner of pebbles where yes I remembered
we took turns at skidding flat ones across
    water
watching them skittering as if alive
and foolishly now I picked another one
but not this time to skim across the
strange unconscious surface

it lies smooth as seagreen surrounded by
the cards and jetsam on our mantel
and Bobby when I look at it
our choirbus again parks itself sideways
the stones rattle under our feet

and your face catches with the pillows
that peculiar reflection of an estate
you are looking saying with someone else's
    voice
I had a good innings
there is a locker your breviary a jug of water
a venetian blind half raised

a load of lighted voices
in harmony:

now is
the hour
when
we must
say goodbye

soon we'll
be
sailing

far across
the sea

while
I'm
away

oh please
remember
me

when I

POUND'S CASTLE
(For Mary)

it seemed easy to catch his soul   *La mia casa*
clean as a gesture in those he loved   *é dura*
to hear his accent implicit as Chaucer's
no other taste shall change this
a world as in Dante's in that name
pronounced by his only daughter
ἀναξιφορμιγξ
πολυτλας much enduring
Pound

his canto castle was richer than a library   *senza ghingheri*
tinkling with its fountain's Etruscan sound
and the gates the stone steps where a mind
    could climb
by turrets walls to an upstairs garden
and see the whole pile sinking into the
    valley of Tyrol
his very room turning to mist to
    thunderforks
vast dazzling strophes cutting through our   *tirata al specchio*
    dead century

of course he waited at the bookshelves
    his age stood there too
tangible as that Gaudier Brzeska head
Eliot Joyce Miller Lewis Cummings Bunting Yeats . . .
all the apes of god a *sensibility*
clothbound with his signature on the fly leaf *E.P.*

or you could come on him reading his poems   *del anima mia*
from the easy chair alongside Dolmetsch's clavichord
(where humbly I did mine own) listen to his voice
booming hieratically through the stone apartments
                                        ▶

A little light, like a rushlight
to lead back to splendour[1]

he challenged you like posters in that room   *é dura*
with the austere table and deckchairs he
    fashioned . . .
a knapsack lugged *anno XXI* from Rome
two portable Remingtons letters cries
out of a past turning into newspaper files
a couple of racquets with broken strings his new
    world
energies everywhere a bulb left on

even the outdoors turned inarticulately his   *dura*
in mountains of silence the mystical fall of a
    gorge
or a slow slow skein unfolding folding in
cloud ideograms just beyond my balcony
    window

the skittering of a *londubh*[2] sly under ivy
became a reminder too just as much as
his vineslopes drifting above the plain
or by a peach tree that water *Smützig*[3] to our
    battlements
floating the bodies of gnats

1: From Canto LXVI by Ezra Pound.
2: Irish for blackbird.
3: 'Dirty' - an expression used by the housekeeper there.

The Italian words are from a poem by Pound's daughter, Mary de Rachewiltz: *My house is lasting/ it has no
ornaments/ a mirror image/ of my soul...*

'EUGENE WATTERS IS DEAD'

somehow we presume our friends will survive
the surest anchor in our shaky universe
and so against flesh and bones was it with Eugene
how could such a spirit so free of his body
crazily generous innocent of bourgie values
so honestly himself so necessary to have around
as everything youthful is   die
who seemed to have no truck with death?
just slip away on us alone? a simple morning phonecall
and *Eugene Watters is dead*

that awful rush as the receiver ticks down
of something over for keeps someone
unique and valiant like the daylight gone

with him our recent past turns priceless flowing
from crowded doors backwards to one half empty pew
in this same St. Michael's where the best man was caught
     coinless
and he laid a shilling on the tray *my worldly goods*

the strange gang of us launching that weekend to the
     wedding party
following his outboard motor up the darkness
I can see this very second a skinny face a life in it turning
the swirl of his Seagull the grin the trapper's cap
and duffel coat of sorts he wore with the next nine years

our first conversation brings me back twenty
to the gate lodge where he squandered an hour on a
     student
and the shapes like ravens among the trees
another to North Frederick Street his Volks playing
twenty minutes' accompaniment too chancy to switch off
— the same jalop that went airborne with a sheet of fibreglass
on the road to Ballinasloe

'Skygrey
in the grey
*   water*
the new life
*   quickens*
tangible
precise grace
in this new

frosted air

these winter
*   wedding*
hours . . .' [1]

and a leaf
from the
bride's
bouquet

all inked
January 1973

the trance
the old fatal —

---

1. Wedding poem by Eugene Watters.

What's the time in your wigwam forest?
Hmm . . . might be Tuesday

now memories scatter in like letters those
readings we did the projects talk nights and Μαργαριτα
below the fields of the world in
his lock house its presence of dream and stone
the smell of water a moon barely shivering
that wide weir mildly continually on the ear
o wine moments never to come again
when hope unlatched the door and took a stool with us
on the flags before an open fire climbed later
up flashlamp stairs to the books a table he carpentered
a cupboard of manuscripts but what are words
without the speaker's *blas*
And a white rose by a wall in Drumcondra
Is simply a shattering thing.

light of morning lies heavy
on the visitors' bedding he spread us
on the huge tarred beam of the sluicegate lodging its
     strangeness
for good his rowboat below the wall
taxiing through drifts of elodia
a white butterfly skipping over new drills
and as we left the swan turning expectantly towards
that cough of a fox . . .

Evgenios high souled your imp smile
has become a needle into the heart is it really true
that you will not lead us across the plank the *flash* on
down the towpath by your reedy mysterious river ever
again?

cyclamen and gladioli linger at the shuttered front
the weir still breaks in quietness it says *Eugene*
and by the lockhouse of Maganey I sat down and wept
having thought you just as immortal

I was wrong was I?

IN FRANCIS LEDWIDGE'S COTTAGE

Ledwidge though I stand here as high in my own
    way
as some of the Stones fans from last week I
didn't have to make this pilgrimage to your
    house
to catch that quiet Meath voice or lift the latch
into your spirit no
the beat of these hills the river and orchard paths

the gables of your short life are in your lines
and we carry them with us everywhere
Lost like a wind within a summer wood
From little knowledge where great sorrows brood

the inherited modesty of being poor
— both Irish and outsider at home
climbs round your words like honeysuckle or the
    distant
singing of a blackbird: the metaphors you
    understood

and we know that we have wandered like you
lonely down summer lanes dreamed along
by the broad flow of emotions too big for us
have returned like you to a kitchen of
certainties quiet and secrets
the Sacred Heart holding out a hand
to family names in copperplate underneath
a shelf of old books the kettle hopping
and games on Sundays up the surviving garden

'I walk the old
frequented ways
That wind around
the tangled braes,
I live again
the sunny days
Ere I the city knew.

And scenes of old
again are born
The woodbine
lassooing the thorn
And drooping Ruth-
    like
in the corn
The poppies weep
the dew

Above me
in their hundred
    schools
The magpies bend
their young to rules,
And like an apron
full of jewels
The dewy cobweb
swings

And frisking in
the stream below
The troutlets make

►

yes 65 years after your world was blown into
   muck we
can call you Frank as your brother did to the end
your life had the common touch we recognise it
for all your moving dandy ways your dickie bow
you never opted out of the Irish experience
you belong to this end of Slane as Yeats to the
   other
where his mind could look through Georgian
   windows
(and indeed they scourged us enough the Anglos
taking — most of them — more than they gave
with that rich tightness which surprises us peasants
Was it needless death after all
For England may keep faith?
surviving like pissibeds)
you died it is true in fusilier's uniform but
this was no Falklands adventure the opposite
poor man idealist—that deadly combination—you
were lured to fight a final war on the barbarian
your private war of love rather than hate one
worthy of your friend Mac Donagh

so coming if I may to myself I prefer
your best poems to Yeats's which over the years
   have
begun to collapse on me like a mansion into words

but since life has a way of shaking the academic
   walls
it is your fragile truths which survive like a
   fanlight

the circles flow,
And the hungry crane
doth watch them grow
As a smoker does
his rings

Above me smokes
the little town
with its whitewashed
   walls
and roofs of brown
And its octagon spire
toned smoothly down
As the holy minds
   within

And wondrous
impudently sweet
Half of him passion
half conceit
The blackbird calls
adown the street
Like the piper of
Hamelin

I hear him, and
I feel the lure
Drawing me back
to the homely moor,
I'll go and close

▶

and I am reminded of a girl who used to carry
the Penguin Yevtushenko in her handbag
dogeared from reading that's how I have packed
some of your poems verses phrases for all the journeys
they have turned shiny as a leather wallet

the mountains' door
On the city's
strife and din.'

for many of us for countless because words are
     your birds
charming listeners unseen across unknown fields
changing things as music does: your poetry
as surely as Keats's say will continue to
enter softly permanently into souls
a kind of sacrament like Patrick's fire
transforming everything

since Ledwidge you had the daring
to make your way alone down that summer lane
down through the flowers and songs down to
     that deeper loneliness
which lies at the bottom of all rambling you found
     the cave
where language can echo reecho shadowing the
     only real
becoming the pure lyric of the only truth we want

that note! the one that can be heard long
     distances
that draws people like us who have travelled
     today
looking for your inspiration
trying to say thanks

---

* *Behind the Closed Eye* by Ledwidge, from the *Complete Poems* (Jenkins, London).

MARTINSTOWN FARE THEE WELL

this part of the world is like a girl
you don't know how to say goodbye
   to although
it's come to that and nobody's fault

I find it hard to believe I
won't be looking much longer out this
small window on my scene
the wall there the house I saw built the
island of sky where one minute it's
rain and windsmoke the next
plover wheeling back to underwhite
whingeing across our shallows
or a swathe of sun cut again
over the roof into my very eyes

ah will the racehorses
clop no more for me along the wall
their anonymous masters turning
   inevitably to glance in
bursting with bad tips?

I can't believe it and no use saying
that everyplace has beauty of its own
that's the very reason I'll pine
a lover in exile trying to remember
that starling sun edging frozen along a
   branch
the life of this room the light kicking off
   cloud
into a cottage musty with old days

of course I'll miss the sights that were
obvious as watercress or the high pine
the little Protestant church abandoned to
   trees

but also neighbours over or back the way
who helped you to believe

and the cut of my road a strangely reas
suring turn
even a bit of wall a gateway onto sheds
I'm still not sure why there should be
excitement in a gap among shadowy bush
down fields that needed no introduction
with friesians scattered to graze forever

— in something new like a flat pool of ligh
or old as a ditch the mist hills I
never needed to reach

MY FATHER

as customary on our Sunday drive we
drove in on this side of The Bay
over the tracks and went bumping down to the edge

out across that space of water the usual car crowds
flashed and glittered under their hotel
which hovered like a church and every so often
a boat would drone past from another world

we dawdled as usual along the path
gone narrow at this stage with bushes with
that feeling of all July coming at you
in midges in weed in wild flowers

he stooped for some meadowsweet handed me a sprig:
it had the last of summer in it that heaviness
of milk just on the turn
by the time we got home it was already drooping
creamy white on the dashboard

but later before leaving I brought it in to him
standing waiting there at the counter
A to hell with it dump it he said
and headed for the steps into the kitchen

LONELINESS

my soul jangles a key
among the uncounted change

now I begin to hear eaveshoots
creaking in heat the cottage
lying in wait

with my mute pictures the
read unread books
shades of other moments
where a record plays

a fake sponge sits damply
the hose coiled in links almost
making bath sounds

August one small fly

and blinds that seem to swell
to speak with your voice

eeeffghhh
ghiiijk
kklmmmnn
ooooo
opqrrsst
uvuvu
vwx
x
x
x
yzabed
yza
abc
bcde
dedede
eeee
dedede
eee
e

A SONG FOR MY FATHER
(1989)

John McCormack: Drawing by Charles Cullen, 1984.

FOR BENJAMIN MOLOISE

(Hanged in Pretoria, Friday 18th October, 1985)

*Life springs from death; and from the graves of patriot
men and women spring living nations. (Padraic Pearse)*

Moloise the world stands
to observe a silence for you
for your people

together we bow our head
around that stadium of suffering
your death now our bereavement your courage
our abhorrence of every repressor

of those who would attempt
to hide freedom in a cloud of teargas
to beat justice to its knees with the *sjambok*
to dangle Africa from a white noose
to bury in quicklime the poetry of youth

and the world's silence runs like blood
it fills their sad swimming pools
seeps into verandahs and through bricks
it hangs on their bullwire it
creeps across the vaults of gold

and deepens
it becomes a scream
it enters our conscience too
with the wood of your coffin the
soft weight Benjamin of your life
as we take turns shouldering your remains
mourning yes but inspired as well at seeing
the spirit being true to itself
an ideal brandished like a burning spear

▶

so that when they hanged you we all became black

the hangman peers and hides and looks at his list

we Irish could have warned him no grave
would go deep enough to hold you
no more than it held Pearse
no more than it can hold any patriot

and though they tried to get rid of you
in the early hours when the world was asleep
the fools!
they did not see your soul breaking over Africa
over the whole earth dawning behind their digging

Benjamin son of days

Root-meaning in Hebrew of Benjamin: *son of days/ of light.*

ECHO'S BONES

(For Sam Beckett on his eightieth birthday)

what have we to do with this hotel
its glass and boutiques and revolving chrome
and black waiter looking for a tip?

where we are sitting again at *doubles* of coffee
conferring like exiles *between the years*
your voice as gently Dublin as Yeats's
and nimbler than hands fallen
like my father's into age

austere and kindly — a monk on his day out
ready to consider any topic for a change
even writers! Joyce and that death mask —
Auden's verse about which we share doubts —
meeting Patrick Kavanagh in Paris —
the fifteen minutes you sat *post-prandium*
when neither you nor Pound uttered a word —
the Paris exhibitions? one shrug
puts them further off than Ireland
(and who could imagine you anyway
stalking peering with a catalogue?)
Company with your own father's 'loved trusted face'
calling to you out of the Forty Foot waves . . .

Marijuana in Ballymahon — there's a poem for you!

▶

and you still surprise me now as you
lean across the marble top with ravelled face
and blue eyes that make us responsible
to quote from *Watt* those lines
'of the empty heart
of the empty hands
of the dark mind stumbling
through barren lands . . .'

and my mind knots again in loneliness
and we are no longer in a coffee bar but somewhere
in the outer space of your words
that almost intolerable silence where
we must try to hang onto some kind of dignity
out in the blinding dark you never shirked

later an embrace and you step off firmly
into streets gone eighty years old
God bless now Desmond

— and you Sam our navigator our valiant necessary
wanderer to the edges of this interpreted world

God bless

DUNNES STORE SALE

big business breathed its hot breath
on my neck as the four of us trolleyed-in
to the dodgems of this whole emporium alive with
preoccupied shoppers yellow-red posters fluorescent
avenues of movers stoppers choosers replacers
mammies without with daddies carrying children
babies in buggies amazed (like me) at the scene
young ones in gear pretending not to notice
stray bargain males
7 p.m. on a Thursday night and all Newbridge
seems to have had the same bright idea
how the hell did I let myself in for this?
10p off marked price
special offer
SALE SALE SALE THE ONE YOU'VE BEEN WAITING FOR
while the sheer quantity of goods moves towards a
quiddity as tantalising as barbecued chickens
making things seem possible teasing our greed into
creeping slyly out between the aisles
going surreal with the jumble of choices:
nappie liners Rioja toothpaste or extra-virgin olive oil?
someone behind the scenes knows
a thing or two about us and speaks from time to time
through an oracle whose utterances cut into
margarine music . . . *was 20.99 now 9.99*
(two women shoot one another a look
they would never waste on a man)
and remember customers . . .
a microcosm with a micro-point of view
more coherent I began to think than my philosophics

looking into a piled trolley ah
was like looking into someone's fridge
it gave the game away we
▶

had got as far as the English queue at the checkouts
where registers bipped and plastic bags filled
up like Santa's when all of a sudden
the scores of squares of wattage down the hangar bli
nked failed without further notice
OUT!
dumping us humans among the lines of shelves
our fingers loosening on the 50p handles *wha-*
that apocalyptic second for which
no one (as always) was quite prepared
everyone everything shoppers assistants goods
plunging reduced

and is death a little like that?

LEARNING RUSSIAN

ever since my soul began growing up
part of it has been learning Russian
the part that knows about winters
the serious part

Mother Russia! despite your goosestep dogma
your tanks trundling across the cobblestones of Europe
betrayed by that great bald mind you
remain for me a peasant in a homemade shawl
offering bread and salt and a place by the hearth

you adopted me orphaned by youth
and gave me Dostoievsky for a big brother
to influence me more than an affair of the heart
he put manners on me changed me quietened me for keeps

you gave me Akhmatova we walked along the Neva
by sombre gardens with covered statues
sat talking on our seat by the Fontanka canal
and her words still follow like sad eyes
keeping me late for everything

Tsvetayeva too both present and far away
makes me phonecalls since she took me in hand
with the sad intensity of an older sister
who knows too much

you gave me poor Mandelstam
oiling his hair at the mirror until
suffering came to take him into custody
and he trudged like Keats into that other country
whose longing speaks straight to the heart

▶

Vladimir Mayakovsky too became a pal
uneasy with energy drinking too much of the future
infuriating friends put out like a dog
and in-between eyeing that stage revolver
with the one real bullet in its chamber

how many times have I shouted down the years
at him at Marina at Yesenin no
not to make ink of their blood not
to give death a hand?

oh and Russia your music! its
unmistakable steppes of vastness unable
to shirk the tragic cold
it rages round the rooms of my student days
more nourishing than any studies I now realise
like the films the few which beat their way through science
towards that *zone* where black and white might at last
burst into full colour into the gold-skied
ikons of longing

Rubyleff Tarkovsky Solzhenitsyn Rachmaninoff Zamyatin . . .
yes so many of your family shared what they had with me
in the hungry years and since they took me in hand I
can still feel that grip like a foreign accent

Holy Mother Russia thank you
for having taught me your language

---

zone: cf. *The Stalker*, a film by Andrei Tarkovsky

SKYLARK

(To the memory of Kieran Collins)

so Kieran old pal your fingering of
the most plaintive music
has been interrupted for keeps the whistle has
slid to the floor in this senseless
exposing silence
and no one else can ever
coax from it your tunes

you have walked out the door
the leather jacket the black western hair
taken for granted with that
precise diffident point of view the shy half laugh
just gone   only this time
you will never slip back join us in a corner and
produce when the mood ripens from your breast pocket
a couple of *penny whistles* no never
play again play play
head to one side out of the way
of the life dancing round the lounge

in notes from the Burren edge the
spirit notes we cannot fully follow
the music beneath the music
tragic hopeful our race moving again in a way in your
spirals knotty interlacings loops and purls of feeling
a skylark over the Irish bogs one
unknowable last time
▶

and now old friend we are left with the pause
to clap when it's too late to call after you
the thanks that never got said to stand in respect
at the true music of what has become your life
sweet as a spring well

put away the whistle I don't want to hear
in death forever my brother I'm saying goodbye

The Skylark: Collins is recognised by musicians as having made this tune his own.

KILBEGGAN DISTILLERY

(For Frank Abbott who reopened it for us)

somehow it's the bloom of the weirs
that first whispers *fugit inreparabile tempus*
even before the foursquare chimney stalk with
LOCKE'S
which rose on so many Sunday afternoons I
even recall the snake-tongued conductor on top
and the bricking within stone the wall clamps the
crúiskín sign above the entrance it's all
only a little more faded now than when we were
                                                                 young

but look! the gentle tumble of the millrace
is turning for us again that high high wheel
lifting its wooden tongues dropping fringe upon
                                                 fringe of
lacewater gracile as First Communion veils

and though it's true the gates open nowadays into
an empty courtyard full of silences
that the vats store only a sodden gloom
or show their ribs like burial ships to newcomers
that engineering is rusting back into iron
abandoned with fluorescent offices
and the bell on the gallery no longer rings quitting
for bosses maltsters coopers labourers all
made redundant by the years

yet light continues through those attic windows
absorbs the dark varnishes worn pine floors
and brings like the spill of water new energies
for all who wish to rebuild and preserve
their own sweet past

whitewater
rushing
over
flowing
falling
falling
falling
splashing
foaming
churning
tossing
foaming
moving
moving
broadening
becoming
continuum
changing
into
years
years
the
years

▶

and the distillery intimates mysteries which can
touch us nourish us with time's peculiar art
the malt you can almost smell! a worker's name
carved in a beam a century ago

and outside in old trees old sunshine by the same
                                                          old river
our mill turns metaphor

fugit: ... *Time flies, irretrievable* (Virgil, *Georgics*)
cruiskin: jar (of whiskey)

FOR FATHER ROMANO ON HIS
45th BIRTHDAY

in you Romano I salute the few
who hand out like bread to others
their ordinary life
and build up block by block
anonymous in the loneliest villages
their chapel to the spirit

who bear witness in remote marketplaces
wearing white against the sun
who make their flesh and blood an angelus
pealing across huts and plots

deeper than bull horn or gunfire
than any saluting officers who imagine they
can bundle truth into a jeep
and stub out freedom with cigarette butts
and build walls higher than the sky
and riddle with foreign rifles
the soul they think they have blindfolded

in you Romano I salute every
missionary of hope
especially if I may the unsung Irish
the ones who have scattered themselves like seed
across forgotten worlds

and when I hear that such as they as you
have ended up in prisons or ditches
I feel as well as rage a fierce pride a
joy of sorts at this reminder
that the resurrection continues

▶

Romano your persecutors will only succeed
in squeezing from your body the blood of Christ
and though they dump you in one compound or another
your soul flies with ease up over
their pathetic cement their money sentries
their rusting barbed wire

flies across the globe makes people like us your family
who would otherwise never have known you

and in your name we join hands
fall into step and sing together
the song of your life

no one can stop our march

Fr. Rudy Romano, a Filipino priest, 'disappeared' in 1985 during the last months of the Marcos regime. He had fearlessly tried to organise poor *campesinos* into demanding living wages and tolerable work-contracts. Witnesses saw him being forced into an army jeep.

PARIS 1985

somewhere beyond comforting a tiny tot
was standing by a stairway in the world
of a department store where I waited

her eyes waiting too
not crying any longer as the shoppers
busied over and back she paid no heed
to the supervisor holding one stray hand

lost for evermore just then a
small planet of solitude
somewhere of abandonment and love no
outsider could hope to reach
loneliness entering her very being
and not a thing we could do

so soon

we delayed
as helpless as she
en attendant

suddenly there came a rush down the steps her
mother her big sister!
she was running she was swooped up
into a whole embrace
the women crying now

and I moved off about my no-business
walking by the counters
yes I admit it hiding a tear

remembering my father

Frère Jacques
Frère Jacques
Dormez vous?
Dormez vous?
Sonnez les matines!
Sonnez les matines!
Ding ding dong
Ding ding dong

HIROSHIMA

(For Akira Yasukawa)

Hiroshima your shadow burns
into the granite of history

preserves for us pilgrims
a wide serious space
where one may weep in silence

I carry in my mind
a glass bullet lodged deep
the memory of that epicentre where
one hundred thousand souls
fused at an instant

and the picture of a soldier
tenderly offering a cup of water
to a burnt child who cannot respond

the delicate paper cranes

---

paper cranes: folded paper birds left at the Children's Monument by children from all over the world

PEACE

(For Seán MacBride)

just to go for a walk out the road
just that
under the deep trees
which whisper of peace

to break the bread of words
with someone passing
just that
four of us round a pram
and baby fingers asleep

just to join the harmony
the fields the blue everyday hills
the puddles of daylight and

you might hear a pheasant
echo through the woods
or plover may waver by
as the evening poises with a blackbird
on its table of hedge
just that
and here and there a gate
a bungalow's bright window
the smell of woodsmoke of lives

just that!

but Sweet Christ that
is more than most of mankind can afford
with the globe still plaited in its own
crown of thorns

▶

too many starving eyes
too many ancient children
squatting among flies
too many stockpiles of fear
too many dog jails too many generals
too many under torture by the impotent
screaming into the air we breathe

too many dreams stuck in money jams
too many mountains of butter selfishness
too many poor drowning in the streets
too many shantytowns on the outskirts of life

too many of us not sure what we want
so that we try to feed a habit for everything
until the ego puppets the militaries
mirror our own warring face

too little peace

HAVE MERCY ON THE POET

(Tengen piedad para el poeta - Pablo Neruda)

— the poet waiting his turn at the Bank Manager's confessional
                                        Lord, have mercy
— the poet hands in trousers in a garage
                                        Christ, have mercy
— the poet filling-in his Tax life
                                        Lord, have mercy
— the poet at the aluminium entrance to the supermarket
                                        Christ, have mercy
— the poet opening one more envelope of verses
                                        Lord, have mercy
— the poet hemming and hawing to friends' questions
                                        Christ, have mercy
— the poet haranguing an audience of 17
                                        Lord, have mercy
— the poet *holding down a steady job*
                                        Christ, have mercy
— the poet pausing at the bestsellers rack
                                        Lord, have mercy
— the poet in a student's pullover
                                        Christ, have mercy
— the poet exaggerating his indifference
                                        Lord, have mercy
— the poet tearing life into the wastepaper basket
                                        Christ, have mercy
— the poet scrounging down the jewelled road
                                        Lord, have mercy
                                        Christ, have mercy

DARAUF

although it's June the ring
on my backdoor feels cool as a
                              coffin's

and there's movement against the
                              ditch a
sizzle on the flat roof ah

rain slinks around the glass kitchen
beading on a pane as I shave runs
glugs sweetly into the gutters by
the last of the flowers

where our blackbird forages peeks in
cheeky as on that night while
droplets go sliding colourless form
little lakes on the folding table
where we ate where the glass held
                              sunset
where you were
your hands your
silver fingers

where the retinae focus intently
they will see the object even
                              afterwards
and an amputated limb I'm told
twinges occasionally

that's how you
linger

words

YOUNG GIFTED — AND UNEMPLOYED

guilty of being unemployed we	*jobbb*
saunter abreast against	*polyp*
shopwindows the male male street	*afternoon*
arms folded like mothers	*job*
our chat as wilful as	*herm*
two earrings in one ear	*herm*
the denim of our youth	*loss*
swelling with a salmon thigh	*oh*
	jobbb
you'd hardly guess our secret	*androg*
if you hit on us down town	*C and I*
in a dole coffeeshop off Main Street	*polyp*
schoolgirls who have left school	*androg*
giggling at a fella chasing a	*herm*
wasp round our table	*androg*
that you should be so lucky!	*afternoon*
	loss
or gathered outside a disco in the lightfall	*loss*
of a glass hotel with army bouncers	*loss*
	exiled
or staring into the near distance	*at home*
while months pass in parents' voices	*job*
and interview queues for interviews	*polyp*
and photocopying C.V.s	*dole*
and hitching alone to the rainy city	*home*
and prelim courses like demo tapes	*job*
and weekend waitressing for tips	*why*
our wage a bottle of house wine	*why*
and parttiming at filling stations topping up	*jobbbb*
middleaged Ireland's cars	*dole*
the one who goes to get the petrol stamps	*herm*

▶

the face in the booth as tyres mutter   *androg*
pissoff pissoff   *C and I*
                                                     oh

we babysit Friday nights   *secure*
trying to read *Woman's Own* after the central   *job*
heating clicks off   *why*
Just one day at a time   *dole*
Sweet Jesus   *herm*
yes it can all turn Country-and-Irish   *hermmmm*
and sometimes we are only pillion passengers   *androg*
                               roaring   *drog*
down the *B and B* roads   *drog*
and sometimes we can feel a   *drogggg*
Dallas weariness in our bones   *polyp*
                                                     WHY

and something is starting to die   *aaaaaaannnnndroooooooggggg*
                                            joooooooooooooooooooooooobb
but never you mind! the morning's   *sssssssssssssssssssssecuuurrrre*
                          ours   *secsecsecsecsecsecsecsecsecc*
we'll swing into it in a gear gang   *ah morning morning*
young young young one last time   *of a day that*
and sometimes unemployment's   *turned*
                         another high   *out*
on which we float and don't give   *different*
                         a damn
about adults waiting with the washup

B and B: Bed and Breakfast houses, offering lodging
C and I: Country-and-Irish music, a rough beast, born middleaged
herm / androg: creatures of doubtful sex

SEQUENCE: A SONG FOR MY FATHER

1

I chanced on a photo

my father in shirtsleeves
standing by the greenhouse

on so relaxed a summer's day
no one bothered to pose
least of all the dandelions

and my mother saying something to Kate
who wonders with the yellow roses

the privet hedge we cut down since looks lovely
a doll lies forever in the sun

and I can almost smell the dinner
see our folding chairs and table the
other side of my camera

the red serviettes blowing

IX

I threw down into the glaury sticky grave
one daffodil from the spring of 1985

tossed it out from me saw it
bump against a freshly dug wall

and with it part of myself
my youth the good times and middling since
the matches the trips to Dublin
deals the shop our walks at *The Bay*
agreements disagreements many and many a laugh
christmases and gatherings and our last weeks
a dying hand

the wet clay of our jumbled loving past

I never saw it land

---

glaury: from Irish 'glár' - watery mud

XV

couple of weekends afterwards I
made that heart-sinking turn again

and up the drive to the entrance
which felt different already without my mother's
yellow rusty Toyota in place

climbed the questioning staircase stepped
down that landing of unhealthy light
into the corridor the bittersweet
gripping my bagful of thanks

beside the Unit our room lay open
empty as the wardrobe

I looked out its window at the fields
the cattle indifferent as before
the cloud houses where other lives were lived
a familiar knifeblade of lake
and the end of the daffodils beside
the road to the world

everything
pretending to be

XVI

month's mind: a small group
along the top two pews of an empty church

and in the epistle Gallio a pro-consul
tells the Jews hounding Paul to feck off
mind their own bleddy business
tough customer the type
that always amused my father

our remnant goes up home

and as we pour tea and try to act normal he
sits to the table his usual place
says *no tomatoes for me*

only he doesn't

we have been
transubstantiated into the past

and even the past is dying

XVII

Cornamagh

living avenues of gravel
leading here
leading there

someone in the distance

the box hedge trimmed
and beeches in a whisper
as when he brought me down
to see this plot

a street of shadows
going to his sunken grave
our bouquets stripped to wire

and leaves like years
lodged in the sodden grass

I do not weep with my mother
standing at McKenna's monument

only his poor tired body
lies here under the trees
only his shaggy eyebrows and white
hair
his eyes no longer curious
the lip he would clench at us
exactly as my small daughter does
his hands that gave the game away

my father is elsewhere

PENINSULA
(1991)

Photograph by Liam Lyons

FARMER NEAR SYBIL POINT

folded-in on himself like the peninsula
unlonely although
full of an unreachable **gloom**
he heads through a gate under

mountains of no illusion

COOSAKNOCKAUN

utter stillness
of one small boat glimpsed out
off the cliffs
on top of the incomprehensible sea

I am an outsider

THE GREAT BLASKET

its authority
slowly drew us in

but the slipway was in moss
those proud cottages sagging
inwards like Irish and

the winds of Europe
blew through blank windows

O Criomhthain
Peig
Muirís O Súilleabháin

I waited on a cliff-height for
for some sign from mainland Ireland

began to understand why mediocrity
never became the norm out here
where existence is an exile

mist islands
a feel of the tremendous
sea through the currach's skin

the imaginary crash of surf
whitening in the distance

cold of a summer morning

and nothing but elements
to add to a quarter century

▶

past *An Tráth Bhán* icy waters
still coursed through the Sound and
over the ships of history

dear dear place
empty in the last mild collapse
of a once-great Gaelic vision
which persisted into our time

IN JOHNNY GRANVILLE'S HOUSE

I am awakened by seaside brightness
raging through blinds the chill an

echo in light

when I glance out the kitchen door
there's a promontory of raw morning
with canyons of space blue distance rock
the white of an egg

I would drive more than 200 miles
for such a breakfast

DINGLE

somehow it never became a *resort*
but kept with its lanes that
puzzling Kerry handshake

the owner of a small supermarket
pointing directions with his butcher's cleaver

carnival of rain

a fishmonger's closed door

waves jumping beyond pubs and masts
at a hulk abandoned like the season

the silo of ice and
tenuous female streets
where ghosts of tourists
stalk without cameras

MINARD CASTLE

and everyone in the car was weary
so why should I drive that far
to poke around its rectangular hulk and peer
into the fifteenth century?

and why did it does it still insist
on rising with hopeful boulders
four storeys in my mind
until I no lover of things military
must go in under the murder hole
to walk around it with words?

a whisper from ancestors
like those whose Drogheda skulls
were unearthed recently clubbed-in?

resisting holding here among their elemental
sky and the searoll the high distances the
cawing of mortality

catching its energies I became aware
of hardy Kerry eyes observing
behind a slitted ope its ingoing
a crack in time
                    ►

Hussey and his lost garrison

I want to look at those sad faces
listen to their Irish try
to hear what they take for granted

to measure things against the heavy keep
as Cromwell's cannons trundle nearer

and pewter bullets whirr and sink

---

pewter: when the native garrison ran out of lead, they used pewter for bullets

BOITHRIN

a pause between showers and it
sends its stone echo uphill

the weathered red of galvanise belongs
and the shed with an upper door for hay

moss velvet on ancient walls

steam meanders from the culvert flags
the fresh green pats of the cows

teck a stonechat hesitates *teck teck*
holding this saturated moment

and the farmhouse eavesdrops on
a stranger's step

Bóithrín/boreen: Irish for, lane

TOURISTS

the retired farmer who
tried to get us the key after midnight

looks over from his morning bungalow
laughs gives a wave and goes in

with that delighful
Kerry delay

rucksacks cars cameras sunglasses
revv into the landscape

never to be loved
among these eternities

DUN AN OIR
A SEQUENCE
(for Michael Murphy and Eileen Dunne)

A Dhia atá fial, a thruath na mbeannachta,
Féach na Gaeil go léir gan bharanta....*
Fear Dorcha O Mealláin *An Díbirt go Connachta*

1

five ships at anchor
pinnaces over
the ropes of water

a galleon foaming in
its Papal ensign slapping
with hope to the silent Irish
watching from cliffs

from centuries

Dún an Oir in Smerwick Harbour was the site of a massacre of six hundred men, women and children in 1580
after a Papal expedition of Spaniards (mainly) Italians and Irish surrendered to Lord Deputy Grey.
God who are generous, compassionate with blessings
see how the Irish are all dispossessed ...
from *The Banishment to Connaught*, 17th Century poem by O'Mealláin).

11
under no flag
their weapons surrendered the surrounded
very ragged and a great part boys
reason in the wrong languages
por favor por favor
per favore
discovering their despair

as Ireland will for many a lifetime
from English soldiery fixing bayonet
testing the knot

no man no woman no crying child
will be allowed wriggle out
the inlet will do for pithead

weasel-eyed Raleigh leads a young girl
back to the fold
Oh cruel Time, which takes in trust
Our youth, our joys, and all we have
the looting and drinking is almost done
and drunken anger closing-in

and already the ropes are out
and already the swords are swishing
and steel thrusts into the screams
and hammers thud from the forge
where they brought Father Moore

▶

---

very ragged ... letter from Sir Richard Bingham to Walsingham, 1580
Oh cruel ... from *Nature That Washed Her Hands In Milk* by Sir Walter Raleigh (1552-1618)

no that is not the screeching of gulls
no that is not the pleading of the wind

Grey takes his daily constitutional
bringing Zouche and Bingham for company

occasionally they stop as he make a point

and back at his quarters
he gazes at thumb and forefinger
searching for a word

111

you can feel it still
the desolation

of Spaniards Italians as they realised
death had sailed from home
which they will never see again

of native Irish exiled by suffering
muttering stoic *Ar nAthairs*

of women and children encircled by
Grey's faith and *Raleigh's mercy*

you can hear the blades mowing
the sound a head makes or a throat
the thumping muffled by bone

listen
sand files back from round the stone

and there are other presences that shall not escape

Elizabeth's ready generals her soldiers
so prone to *revelling and spoiling* before
getting down to serious business
Elizabeth's grim Deputy so strong of stomach
Elizabeth's pet poet

▶

Ar nAthairs : *Our Fathers*
revelling ... letter from Bingham to Lane, 1580

bald Elizabeth herself
a gloss on *this late enterprise performed by you
so greatly to Our liking*

after the few women had been raped
one more time and decapitated like chickens
after the last head tossed to the cove
and body unroped heeled out
after the final child sworded-through
the sledgehammers dropped did
Raleigh and Macworth escort Grey
across the spongy land
to inspect the remains of the agreement and
did they advert to the wint'ry beauty as Phoebus
hid his wat'ry locks beyond the
shoals of corpses?

in the crying of these fields

---

this late enterprise ... letter from Queen Elizabeth to Lord Grey, 1580

IV

féach an rópa ar an gcroch !
a Thiarna Dia
táid chun sinne Gaeil a chrochadh
a Dhia a Dhia a Mhuire na ngrást
agus na mná? agus na páistí

*Papish dirt! here
try this English rope for size*

heave ho my hearties

    Daidi! a Dhaidi
    lig leis más é do thoil é
    níor dhein se tada
    achainím impím ort
    ná cuir an rud sin air
    ná ná ná ná ná
    sin é mo Dhaidi
    mo Dhaidi

        in ainm an Athar agus an Mhic
        agus and Spioraid Naoimh
        creidim i nDia
        an tAthair Uilechumhachtach
        Cruthaitheóir neimhe agus talmhan

*dove é San Giuseppe?
che cosa face
ho studiato a Firenze
mi padre! mi madre!
perché perché perché?*

bhí cónaí ar mo shinsear annseo
le fada an bhliain
ach anois tá mo shráidbhaile dóite
mo mhóinfhéar dubh agaibh
mo chlann scaipithe
is cuma liom bás nó beatha
níl sa bheatha a dfhág sibh againn
ach sórt báis
fágaidh mé an saol dorcha seo
gan bhrón

    an Gearaltach mallaithe
    cá bhfuil an cladhaire anois?
    agus and t-Iodáileach olc sin
    bhain se an claidheamh d' ár lámhaibh
    agus sháith sé Trócaire Raleigh ina áit
    tá mo phort seinnte fiú gan troid

        go tapaidh a Mháire bhig
        síos leat ar an gcosán san
        le taobh na h-aille
        sar a dtagann siad thar n-ais
        ag lorg níos mó díghe
A Dhia atá fial, a thruath na mbeannactha,   slán agus beannacht a mhúirnín
Féach na Gaeil go léir gan bharanta   go tapaidh ! cloisim arís iad
        ag iompar na gcorpán

    ►

For translations see Appendix, p. 178

madre de Dios! mira los Irlandeses
señor señor por favor
tengo monedas para ti

Irish shit! fight back would you?
now how do you feel eh?

éist éist
tá an dorchadas mór ag caoineadh

éist leis an speachaíl
na daoine bochta
táim-se ag dul as mo mheabhair
tabharfaidh mé léim amach ó'n aill
b'fhearr liom é sin
ná an céasadh uafásach seo

m'fhear m'fhear
tabhair dom m'fhear breá
a shaighdiúirí caoine
ná ná déanaigí é sin
a Mhuire a Mháthair Dé

déan trócaire
déan trócaire
tóg do láimh uaim-se
a Dhia a Dhia

trócaire trócaire trócaire
níl aon arm agam
cad mar gheall ar an gcomhrac?

fan in aice liom a Thomáis a mhic
ní chuirfidh siad isteach ort
creid ionnam
ní ligfidh mé dóibh é
fan liom a leinbh
fan liom-sa

is athair mé mar thú féin
tógaigí bhur lámha díom
cladhairí
neamh-fhir
madraí
tabhair mo phíce dom a mheatacháin
agus déanfaidh mé troid leat
a phéist
go h-Ifreann libh go léir
a Iosa Críost
cabhraigh liom anois

eviva il Papa!

go saoraidh Dia Eire bhocht

V

dispatch penned for the Deputy in
most careful and beautiful italic
Spenser gets down to *the writin'*

in his bivouac he explores
vellum and chair the canvas wall

across a dying november evening
he can discern hardly any screaming now

he dips quill begins to scratch
a phrase into the *Teares of the Muses*

And ye Faire Ladie th'honor of your
daies
And glorie of the world, your high
thoughts scorne,
Vouchsafe this moniment of his last
praise
With some few silver dropping teares
t'adorne:
And as ye be of heauenlie off-spring
borne,
So unto heauen let your high mind aspire
And loathe this drosse of sinful worlds
desire.

---

most careful ... description by Renwick, editor of *A View of the State of Ireland* by Spenser (1596).
right column: Spenser, from *The Ruines of Time*. (These lines are addressed Queen Elizabeth I).

V1

blood on the grass
horror under the fern

evening swings like a body
the mist is cold as steel
death stinks from the bay

no bird will sing
at Ard na Caithne
nor no wave wash
away what remains

éist éist
the cliff screams at Ard na Ceartan

éist... listen

EPILOGUE

out the window of my study
Papel rasgado de um intento
a leaden March morning gives
and blue tatters show
there's a crow gawking from a bare tree
a volley from an unseeable blackbird

and for no reason I remember Kerry
the long road of stillness
An Fheóthanach shivering with daylight
the perspective to the Sisters
mist heights a view of abandoned ocean
somebody's voice coming a long way
life draining from a hill

landscape of tragic faces
where time fades to eternity

that great grey movement
over us all

Papel ... The torn paper of a draft : from a poem by Fernando Pessoa.
 An Fheóthanach: place name, Feohanagh.

NOTES FOR DUN AN OIR

POEM IV (page 170)
Left column : (1) look at the rope on the gallows/ Holy God/ they're going to hang us Irish/ God God, holy Mary/ and the women and children too (2) Daddy oh Daddy/ please let him alone/ he did nothing/ I beg I beseech you/ don't put that thing on him no no no no no/ that's my daddy/ my daddy (3) where is San Giuseppe (the leader)?/ what is he doing?/ I have studied in Florence/ my father my mother!/ why why why? (4) damned Fitzgerald/ where is the villain now/ and that evil Italian/ he took the sword out of our hands/ and gave us *Raleigh's mercy* instead/ I'm finished without even a fight (5) (Epigraph from beginning of Sequence)

Right column: (3) The Sign of the Cross and start of Apostles' Creed (4) my ancestors lived here/ long years/ but now my tillage is burnt down/ my meadow blackened by you/ my family scattered/ I don't care whether I live or die/ the life you left us/ is only a kind of death/ I'll leave this dark existence/ gladly (5) quickly, little Mary/ go down that path/ by the side of the cliff/ before they come back/ looking for more drink/ goodbye and God bless you darling/ quick! I hear them again/ carrying the bodies.

(page 171)
Left column : (line 1) Mother of God! look at the Irish/ sir, sir, please/ I have money for you (2) listen listen/ the great darkness is crying (3) my husband my husband/ give me my grand husband/ good soldiers/ don't do that/ Mary Mother of God (4) help help help! I'm unarmed/ what about the truce?/ help me/ I'm like yourself/ take your hands off me/ cowards/ non-men/ dogs/ give me my pike villain/ and I'll fight you/ snakes / to hell with the lot of you/ Jesus Christ/ help me now

Right column: (line 2) listen to them kicking/ the poor people/ I'm going mad/ I'll jump off the cliff/ I'd prefer that/ to this awful crucifixion (3) mercy mercy/ take your hand off me/ take your hand off me/ oh God God (4) stay with me Tom my son/ they won't touch you/ believe me/ I won't let them/ stay with me child/ stay with me (5) long live the Pope (6) God save Ireland

INDEX OF TITLES AND BOOKS

INDEX OF FIRST LINES

owned by some neighbours you never meet, 17

préacháin go glórach ar an díon íseal, 96

remember the dew how white it was?, 66
riveted girders blur of carfaces, 33

saying goodbye for the umpteenth time the mind, 91
she told him then how the rabbit, 30
she would waddle out from their stone kitchen, 87
so Kieran old pal, 135
some days leave a recognisable, 76
somehow it's the bloom, 137
somehow it never became a resort, 175
something you say unthinkingly sometimes, 29
somewhere beyond comforting a tiny tot, 141
Sweetheart the night is growing old, 28

Tá gaoth ag séid ar mo shaol monuar, 95
talk with me love one last time, 148
tatty Wicklow! it surprised me, 114
teal, 25
the appleblossoms waltzed white roses, 47

the light had a strange intenseness, 149
the only weekend before another by-election, 58
the poet waiting his turn, 145
the redheaded schoolboy (farmer's son), 27
the retired farmer who, 176
then we were standing on the top, 24
there is very little I want really, 135
this part of the world is like a girl, 122
through flurries of wind and the rain I, 100
trout feeding along the river, 42
two wee girls, 32

under no flag, 166
under siege no doubt themselves the Guards, 57
up the tunnels of June, 41
utter stillness, 158